# ADVENTURES iN FAMOUS PLACES

## Packed full of Activities and over 250 Stickers

This little squirrel is hiding in every main sticker scene. Can you find him?

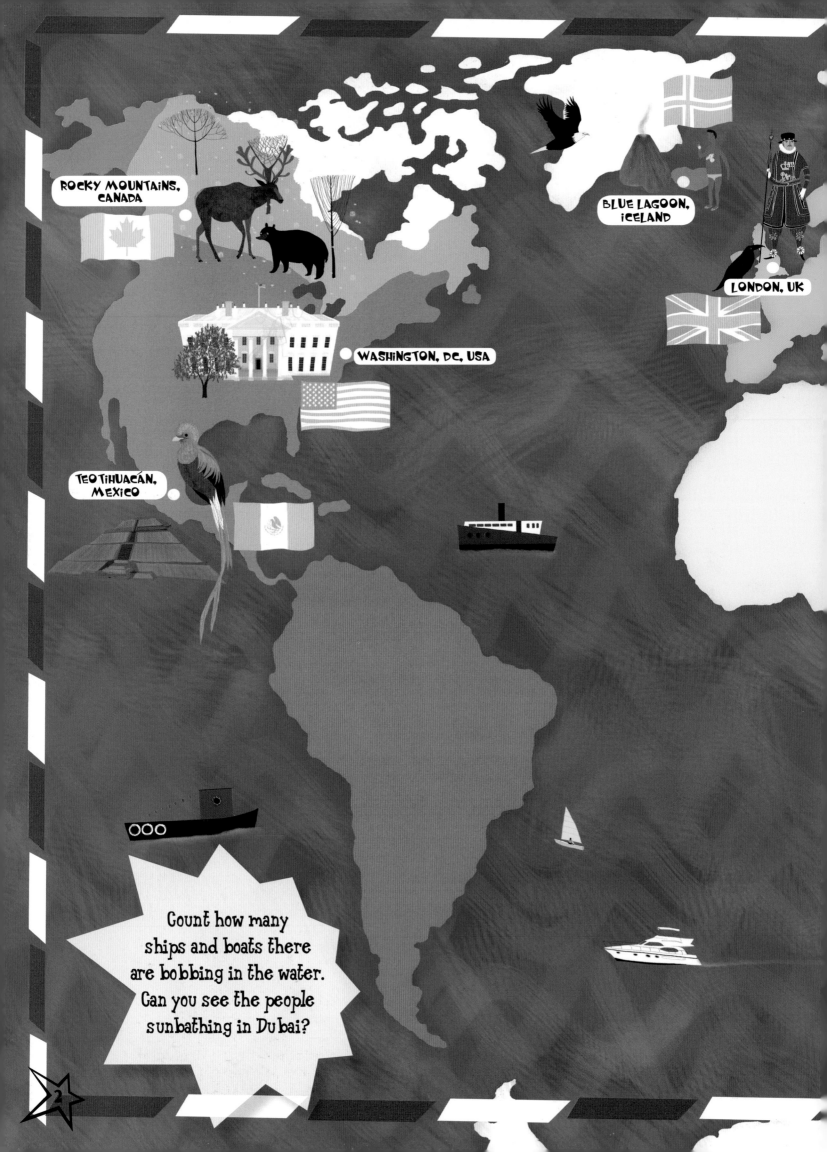

# FAMOUS WORLD

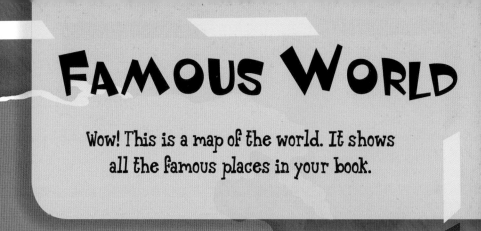

Wow! This is a map of the world. It shows all the famous places in your book.

TAKAYAMA, JAPAN

DUBAI, UAE

UDAIPUR, INDIA

There's a flag for each famous place you'll be exploring. Find the matching stickers at the end of your book and stick them in the right places.

ADDO ELEPHANT NATIONAL PARK, SOUTH AFRICA

ULURU, AUSTRALIA

# READY TO GO!

Make an adventure pass to explore famous places!
Write your name and age, draw your picture, and then add your country stamp stickers.

## MY FAMOUS ADVENTURE PASS

Name
.................

Age
.................

Draw your face here.

Stick your country stamps here.

## FAMOUS PLACES POSTCARD

Draw something famous on the postcard. Then write the name of someone to send your postcard to.

Don't forget to draw a stamp!

Hi and bonjour

CANADA

Canada is famous for Justin Bieber, the CN Tower, and a multitude of moose, maple trees, and Mounties.

Moose are huge deer with wide antlers and big hooves that work like snow boots. Beware – a moose is on the loose!

It's cold! This girl needs a warm, woolly hat and scarf. Can you give her a hot drink too?

Mounties are policemen who often ride horses and wear campaign hats with a flat brim. Their uniforms are called red serge – easy to see when they surge ahead.

5

Wildlife in the Rockies includes cougars, red squirrels, bighorn sheep, black bears, grizzly bears, and bald eagles. Can you find any of them here?

# THE ROCKIES

are a vast mountain range crossing from Canada into the United States. A train from Vancouver takes passengers through spectacular scenery to towns like Jasper and Banff.

# iCE SKATERS

It's important to wear layers of warm clothing when skating on frozen lakes and rivers!

Can you make the skaters' clothes stand out in the snow?

Paint the woolly hats red and the scarves green.

Hello

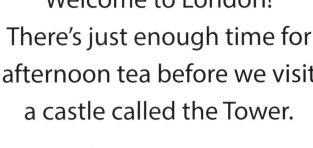

# UNITED KINGDOM

Welcome to London! There's just enough time for afternoon tea before we visit a castle called the Tower.

Police officers in the UK wear tall, pointed helmets with crisp black tunics. They are also called Bobbies, after Sir Robert Peel, who started the police force.

Londoners speak 300 languages, so you can always find someone to talk to, whatever your nationality.

Stick your stamps on the letter and parcels before you send them.

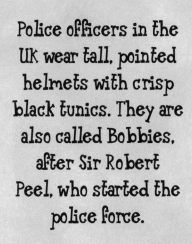

Her Majesty The Queen

Buckingham Palace

LONDON

SW1A 1AA

MR HATT
THE BURJ KHALIFA.
MOHAMMED BIN RASHID BLV.
DOWNTOWN DUBAI
U. A. E.

To MIA & ELLA
THE LAKE PALACE HOTEL
PO BOX 5  LAKE PICHOLA
UDAIPUR  313001
RAJASTHAN
INDIA

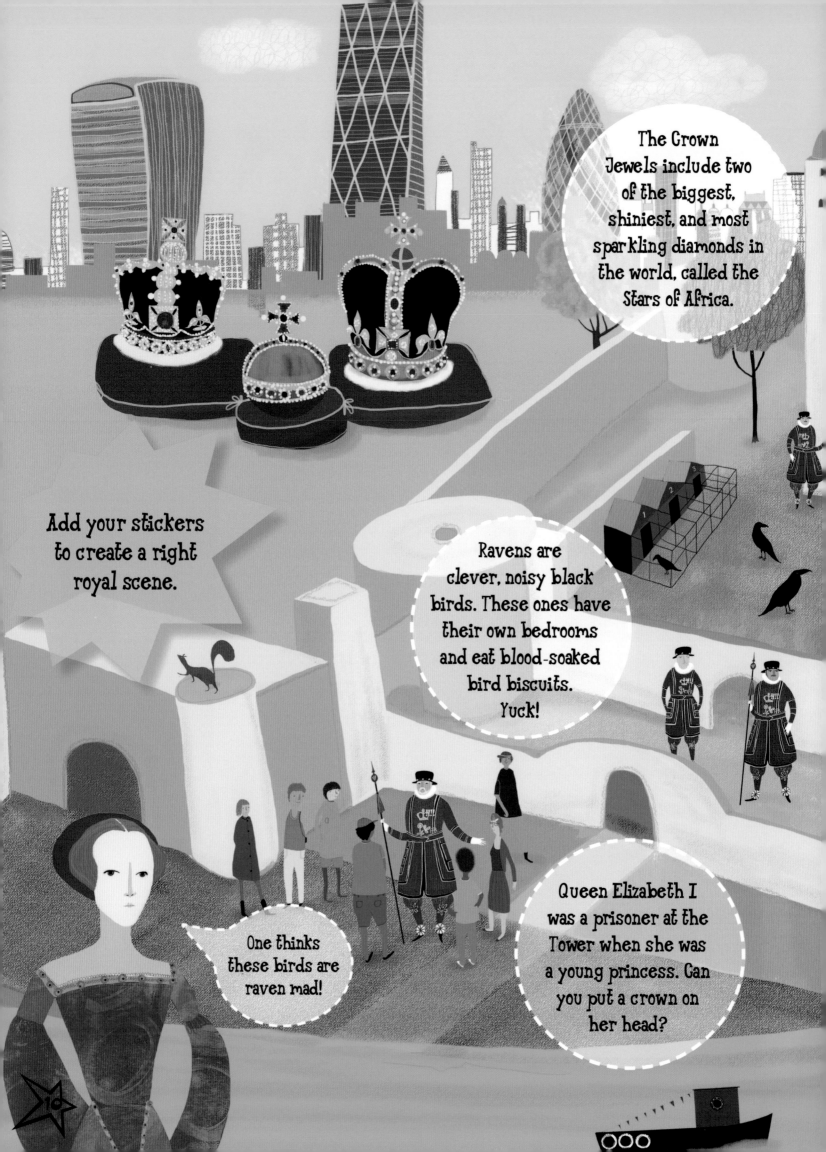

# TAKING THE BUS

There are more than 8,000 buses in London, transporting people across the capital city every day. Nearly all of them are bright red.

Sightseeing buses are open on top to provide a better view of London, but some people prefer to sit downstairs and keep warm.

You meet a variety of people on London buses, from local residents to visiting tourists. You also hear many different languages. All aboard!

Double-decker buses have steps to the top deck. The old-style Routemaster bus has a driver and a ticket collector called a conductor. Can you paint the bus red and decorate all of the passengers?

Halló

Ride a horse across rocky black lava fields. It's time to rock and roll!

¡CELAND

Welcome to the land of fire and ice, where the summer sun shines all night long. Iceland is famous for icy glaciers, erupting volcanoes, seabirds called puffins, and the spectacular Northern Lights.

When a volcano erupts, it produces ash clouds and burning-hot lava that turns into black rock as it cools down.

Use your stickers to feed the puffins some fish.

Puffins are funny-looking black and white birds with decorated beaks and bright orange legs.

13

**THE BLUE LAGOON** is a geothermal spa, or a great big outdoor bath, where people swim in the middle of dramatic volcanic lava fields.

Add lots of people to bring this busy lagoon to life.

The Blue Lagoon welcomes more visitors every year than the entire population of Iceland. Imagine all those people sharing your bath!

The lagoon water looks bright blue and is filled with rich minerals called silica and sulphur. It's one smelly pool!

# iCELANDiC HORSES

Icelandic horses, brought by the Vikings many centuries ago, are the oldest and purest breed in the world. They are very calm and friendly.

Although small, these horses are powerful enough to carry big adults across rivers, lava fields, and icy glaciers.

They can walk, trot, canter, and also tölt, which is a fast walk.

In winter the horses grow beards and their black, chestnut, silver, or spotted coats become long and thick. Can you spot some spotted horses and decorate them?

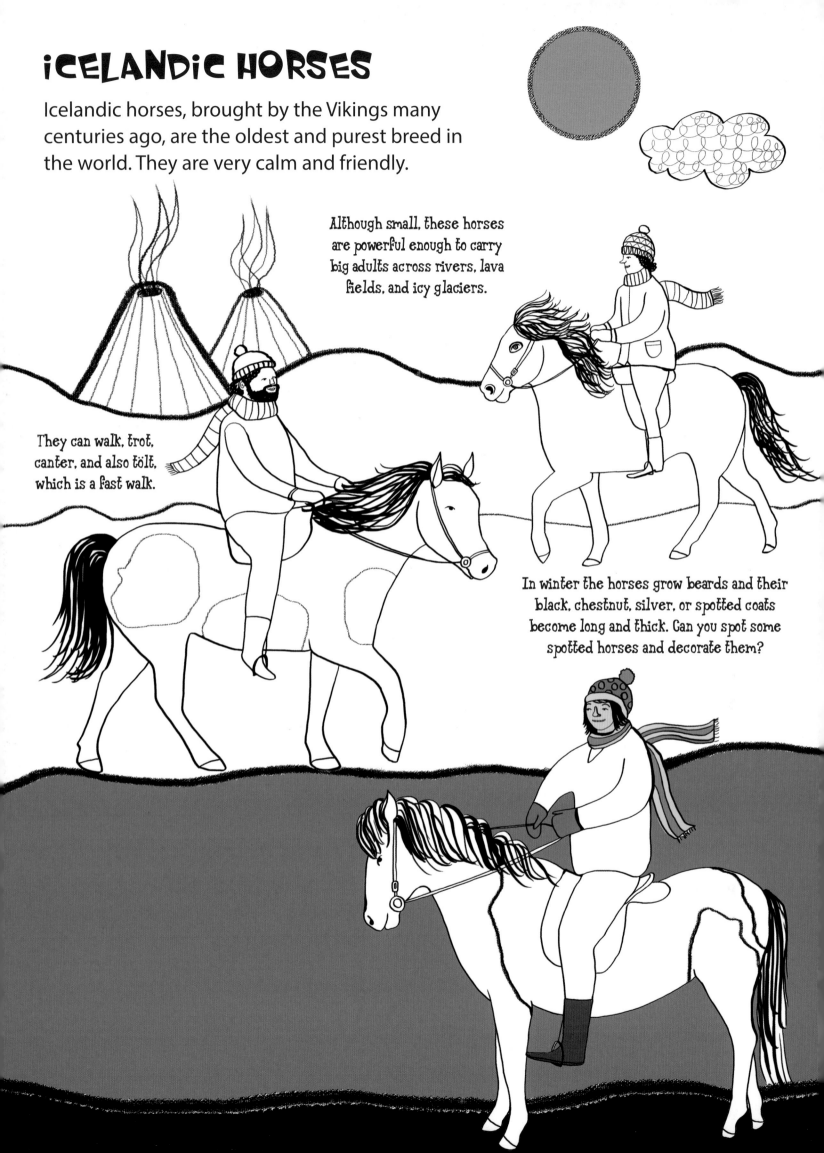

Hola

The Sombrero is a wide straw hat, which creates shade and protects people from the hot Mexican sun.

# MEXICO

Mexico is famous for sombreros, a tasty dip called guacamole, burritos with delicious fillings, and an amazing artist named Frida Kahlo.

Mariachi bands play folk music on guitars, trumpets, violins, and sometimes accordions. The most famous mariachi song, La Cucaracha, will make you wince. Its name means the cockroach!

Frida Kahlo was a painter from Coyoacán, in Mexico. She lived in a bright blue house and painted 55 vibrant portraits of herself.

Give the mariachi musicians a sombrero, shaker, and accordion to help them make Mexican music!

17

The Pyramid of the Moon is surrounded by beautiful buildings. When the Moon shines at night, the pyramid looks radiant.

Choose a place to put your stickers to liven up this Mexican scene.

Pictures of birds and butterflies have been carved onto the columns of Quetzalpapalotl Palace. Its name means a butterfly crossed with a quetzal bird.

The main path between the pyramids is 4 km (2.5 mi.) from end to end. It takes almost an hour to walk its length!

**TEOTIHUACAN,** called the Place of the Gods, is filled with huge pyramids and many other ancient monuments. The city became important to the Aztec people, though it was built before their time.

People climb up 240 steps to the tip of the Pyramid of the Sun. They make a wish and hope the site will give them energy – which they might need to get back down!

# QUETZAL BIRD

The green tail feathers were used for Aztec royal ceremonies. They can be 1 m (3 ft.) long – the average height of a 3-year-old child!

The quetzal is perhaps the most beautiful bird in the world. It lives in the tropical forests of Central America.

**Namaste**

# INDIA

India is home to a beautiful building called the Taj Mahal, sloping green fields where they grow tea, and the Bollywood film studios in Mumbai, where they make musicals.

The Taj Mahal, in Agra, is made from white marble and was built by an emperor in memory of the wife he loved.

Wild tigers live alone in forests. Their striped coats help them hide when they are hunting. Every tiger's stripes are different – just like our fingerprints.

Put some charming snakes in the snake charmer's basket!

# TEA PICKERS

Tea is the world's most popular drink. Tea plants are grown in India, China, and Japan, and workers often pick tea leaves from the plants with their hands. Time to put the kettle on!

Tea pickers are often women. Can you brighten up their hats?

The pickers wear conical straw hats, wide brimmed bamboo hats, or bright woven head wraps.

Hi

# USA

Americans love popcorn, hot dogs, hamburgers, and turkey with cranberry sauce, but there's nothing more American than homemade apple pie.

Americans celebrate Thanksgiving by eating roast turkey with cranberry sauce and mashed potatoes, followed by pecan pie, pumpkin pie and, of course, apple pie. Yummy!

The Lincoln Memorial is a beautiful marble building to remember President Abraham Lincoln. The Washington Monument is a huge marble obelisk, or column, to remember President George Washington.

Add some tomato, cheese, and cucumber to your burger. Don't forget the ketchup!

The presidential helicopter lands on the South Lawn, behind the White House.

The First Lady arranges big parties at the White House. Have you been invited?

Add your stickers to make the White House busy and bustling.

The West Wing of the White House includes the famous Oval Office, where the president works with his team.

**THE WHITE HOUSE,** on Pennsylvania Avenue in Washington, DC, has been the home and office of the United States president and his wife, the First Lady, for more than two hundred years.

Presidential pets have included Clinton's cat, Socks, Obama's dog, Bo, and Kennedy's pony, called Macaroni.

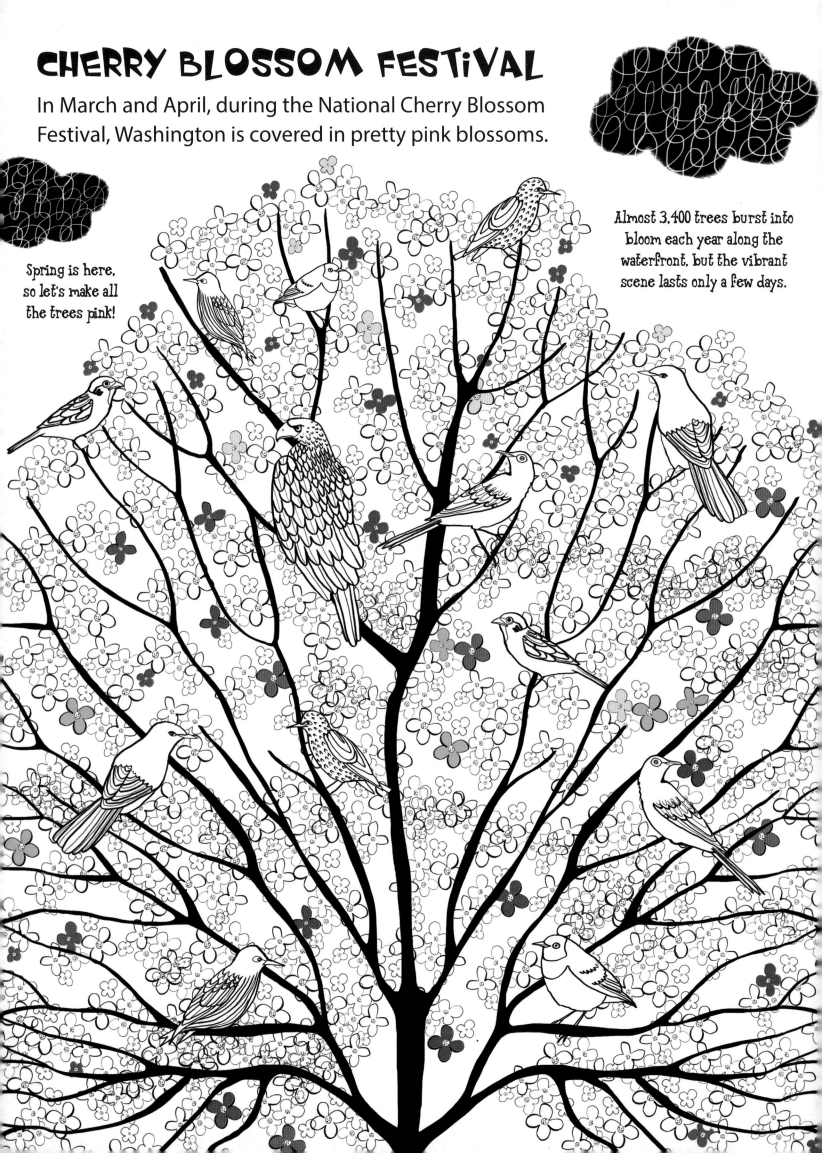

# CHERRY BLOSSOM FESTIVAL

In March and April, during the National Cherry Blossom Festival, Washington is covered in pretty pink blossoms.

Almost 3,400 trees burst into bloom each year along the waterfront, but the vibrant scene lasts only a few days.

Spring is here, so let's make all the trees pink!

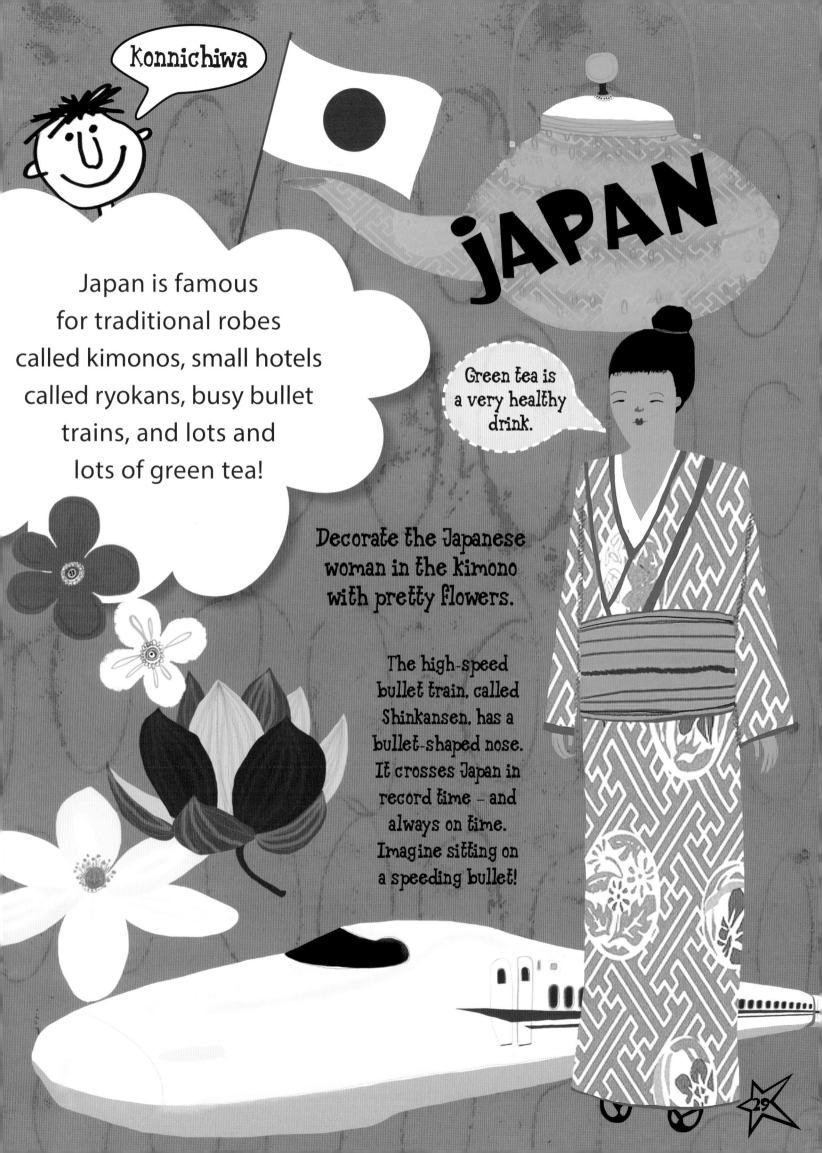

Konnichiwa

JAPAN

Japan is famous for traditional robes called kimonos, small hotels called ryokans, busy bullet trains, and lots and lots of green tea!

Green tea is a very healthy drink.

Decorate the Japanese woman in the kimono with pretty flowers.

The high-speed bullet train, called Shinkansen, has a bullet-shaped nose. It crosses Japan in record time – and always on time. Imagine sitting on a speeding bullet!

29

# THE TAKAYAMA FESTIVAL

The pretty Japanese town of Takayama is filled with quaint houses and lots of breweries. It is best known for a festival held every spring and autumn.

Sannomachi Street, in the old town, is lined with ancient wooden homes, shops, coffee houses, and breweries that make a rice drink called sake.

# SUMO WRESTLERS

Sumo is Japan's national sport. The young wrestlers live together, training for many years.

To put on weight and become enormous, the wrestlers eat lots of meat stew called chankonabe and take short naps.

They wear a belt called a mawashi. The best wrestlers also wear long, embroidered cloths. Can you decorate them all?

The gigantic wrestlers train in silence, but you can still hear them bash into each other. Thud!

**Hallo**

# SOUTH AFRICA

South Africans speak many languages, including English and Afrikaans. The country is famous for shiny diamonds, sandy beaches, huge safari parks, and wild monkeys called baboons.

Dassie rats are pale grey, dark brown, or jet black. Their flexible ribs help them squeeze in between tight rocks.

Make sure the car doors are locked when the baboons arrive. These animals are very clever and very naughty, and they get up to a lot of monkey business!

Give the tourists a ride on the cable car.

Cape Town's flat-topped hill is called Table Mountain. Some people hike up, but there is also a cable car to the spectacular summit.

33

# ADDO ELEPHANT NATIONAL PARK

is home to many wild animals, including over 600 elephants that move around very quietly. Sometimes the herd can be seen but NOT heard!

Elephants drink, wash, and play at the waterhole. When a baby calf gets stuck, its mother helps push it out of the water.

African elephants weigh four times more than a car. They can move silently thanks to their padded feet – just like people wearing slippers.

# THE BIG FIVE!

Everybody comes to Africa to see the so-called big five: elephants, lions, rhinoceros, buffalo, and leopards.

The male lion is the king of the jungle, with a big, hairy mane and huge strength. But he spends all day sleeping – snoring instead of roaring!

The rhinoceros is a plant-eating animal. It has an enormous horn on its head made of keratin, just like our hair and fingernails. Can you paint the rhino and his friends?

# AUSTRALIA

G'day, mate

The Northern Territory is in Australia's rugged Outback. Here you'll find the city of Darwin, Kakadu National Park, and a town called Alice Springs. Look out for some really wild wildlife too!

Kakadu is filled with crocodiles. They leap into the air to catch chunks of meat that are dangled on sticks over the sides of tour boats. Talk about getting snappy!

Add more animals to complete the signs! Watch out for the jumping crocodile!

Dingoes are wild dogs. They have red or gold coats and live in packs of about ten. They don't bark like domestic dogs but instead howl like wolves!

At night there is total darkness at Uluru. The sky is so clear that groups of stars, like the Southern Cross, can easily be seen.

ULURU, OR AYERS ROCK, is in a desert region called the Red Centre. Aboriginal people believe Uluru is a very important spiritual place created in an age called Dreamtime.

There are Aboriginal paintings inside Uluru caves. Outside there are wild dingoes, hopping kangaroos, and long-necked birds called emus that look like ostriches.

# UP, UP, AND AWAY

Hot-air balloons take off from Alice Springs early in the morning to fly people over the Outback.

Can you decorate all of the balloons?

Make them very bright to help people see them from the ground.

As-salaam alaikum

Arabian camels have small hairy ears, two rows of eyelashes to screen them from desert sand, and a single hump on their back.

## DUBAI

Dubai (UAE) has some fantastic attractions, including an indoor ski resort, human-made islands, and a huge automated metro rail system.

A hotel called Atlantis stands on a human-made island in the Persian Gulf. Guests can sleep in underwater bedrooms and swim with sharks!

Add some passengers to the train.

Dubai Metro, with almost 50 stations, is the longest driverless train network in the world, covering 75 km (47 mi.). Hold on tight!

The Jumeirah and downtown areas of **DUBAi** are filled with some of the biggest, tallest, and most expensive buildings in the world.

The Madinat Jumeirah Resort has its own canal system!

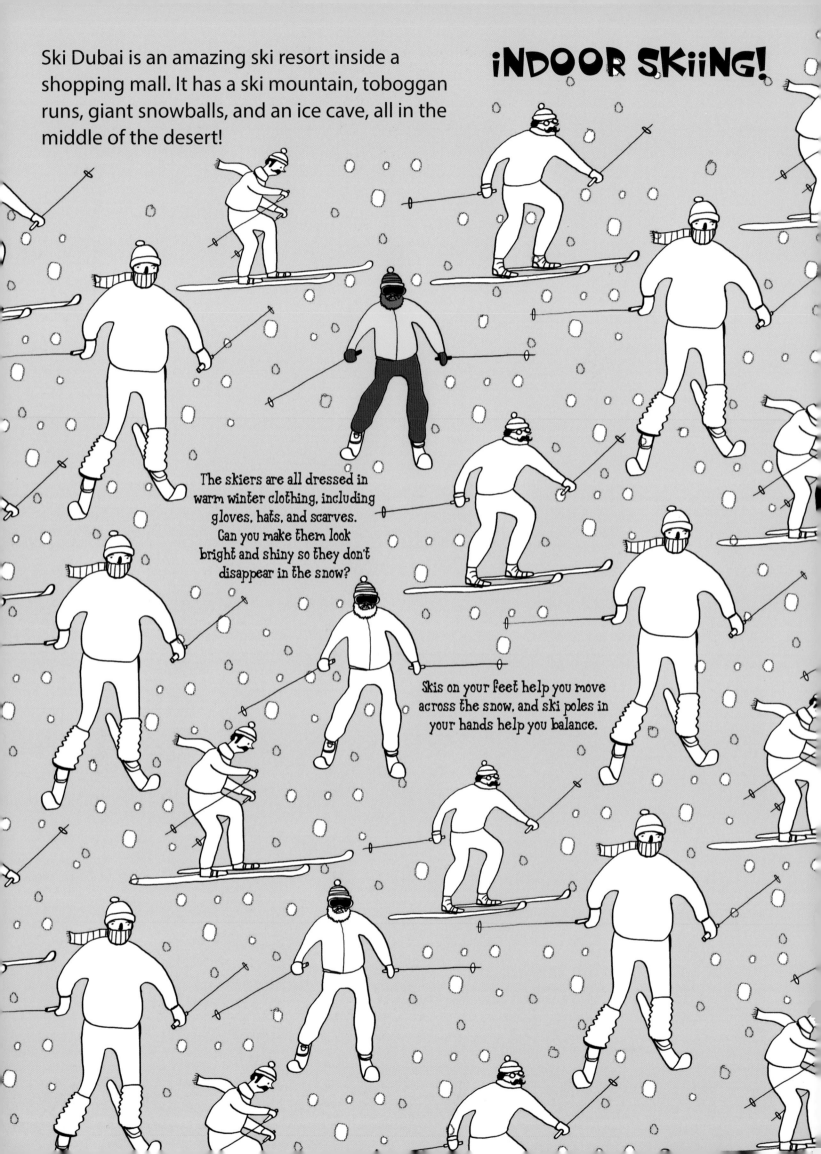

Ski Dubai is an amazing ski resort inside a shopping mall. It has a ski mountain, toboggan runs, giant snowballs, and an ice cave, all in the middle of the desert!

¡INDOOR SKiiNG!

The skiers are all dressed in warm winter clothing, including gloves, hats, and scarves. Can you make them look bright and shiny so they don't disappear in the snow?

Skis on your feet help you move across the snow, and ski poles in your hands help you balance.

# FAMOUS DIFFERENCES

Spot six differences between these two pictures.

**1**

**2**

45

# FAMOUS SHADOWS

Can you match the famous things with their shadows?
Draw a line with a crayon from the picture to its shadow.

# FAMOUS MAZE

Pick your person and see where the path will take them.

# ANSWERS FOR PAGES 45, 46, AND 47

**FAMOUS DIFFERENCES**

**FAMOUS SHADOWS**

**FAMOUS MAZE**

1. The squirrel on the left turns yellow in 2.
2. The moose is facing the opposite way in 2.
3. The black bear disappears in 2.
4. A deer on the right appears in 2.
5. The fox on the right disappears in 2.
6. A little purple bird in the bottom right appears in 2.

1. The safari ranger takes you to look at the rhinoceros.
2. The Yeoman Warder takes you to view the Crown Jewels.
3. The Japanese woman takes you to see a yatai.
4. The tourist takes you to see the Pyramid of the Moon.

Published in March 2015 by Lonely Planet Publications Pty Ltd
ABN 36 005 607 983
www.lonelyplanetkids.com
ISBN 978 1 74360 779 4
© Lonely Planet 2015
Printed in China

| | |
|---|---|
| **Publishing Director** | Piers Pickard |
| **Publisher** | Mina Patria |
| **Art Director & Designer** | Beverley Speight |
| **In-house Senior Designer** | Claire Clewley |
| **Author** | Mark Conroy |
| **Illustrator** | Anne Wilson |
| **Pre-press production** | Tag Response |
| **Print production** | Larissa Frost |
| | |
| **Thanks to** | Lisa Eyre, Jessica Cole |

**Lonely Planet offices**

AUSTRALIA
90 Maribyrnong St, Footscray, Victoria, 3011, Australia
Phone 03 8379 8000 **Email talk2us@lonelyplanet.com.au**

USA
150 Linden St, Oakland, CA 94607
Phone 510 250 6400 **Email info@lonelyplanet.com**

UNITED KINGDOM
Media Centre, 201 Wood Lane, London W12 7TQ
Phone 020 8433 1333 **Email go@lonelyplanet.co.uk**

p2-3 World map

p17 Mexico

p4 country stamps

p13 Iceland

p9 UK

p5 Canada

p21 India

p25 USA

p33 South Africa

p29 Japan

p37 Australia

3d model

p41 Dubai

**p6-7 The Rockies**

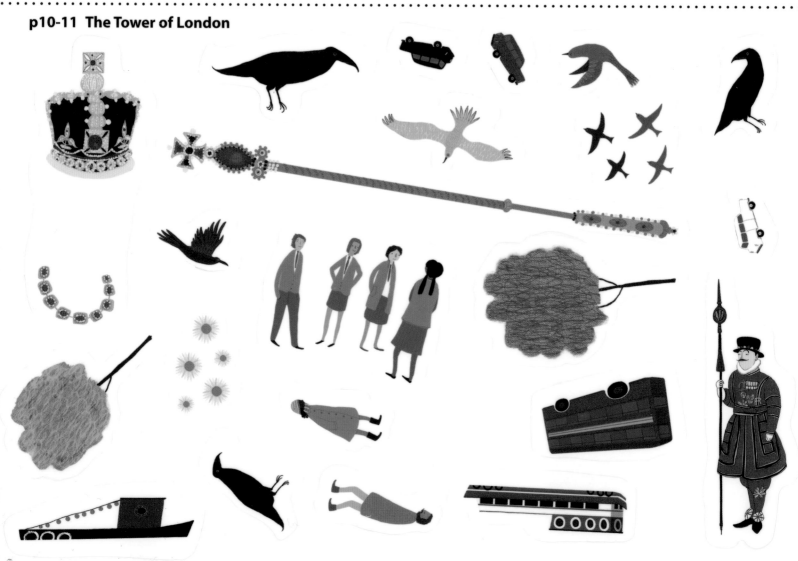

**p10-11 The Tower of London**

**p14-15  The Blue Lagoon**

**p18-19  Teotihuacan**

p22-23 Udaipur

p26-27
The White
House

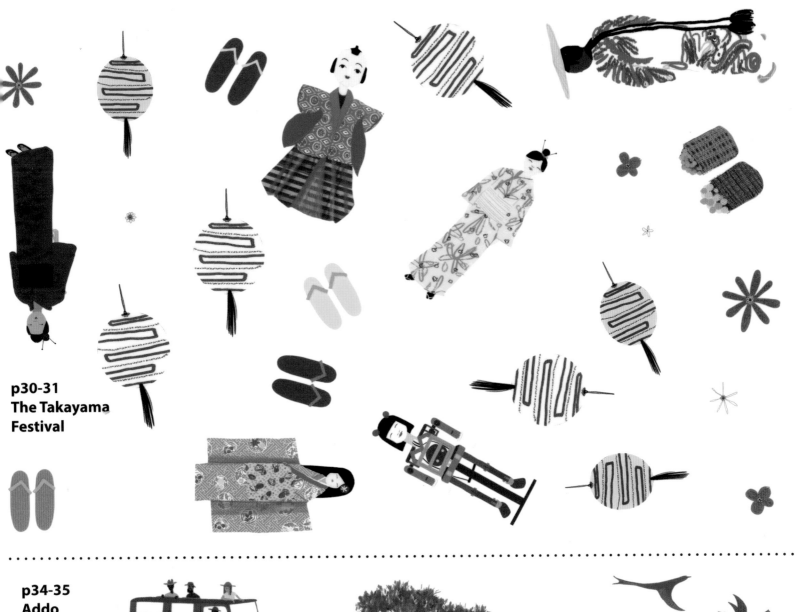

**p30-31
The Takayama
Festival**

**p34-35
Addo**

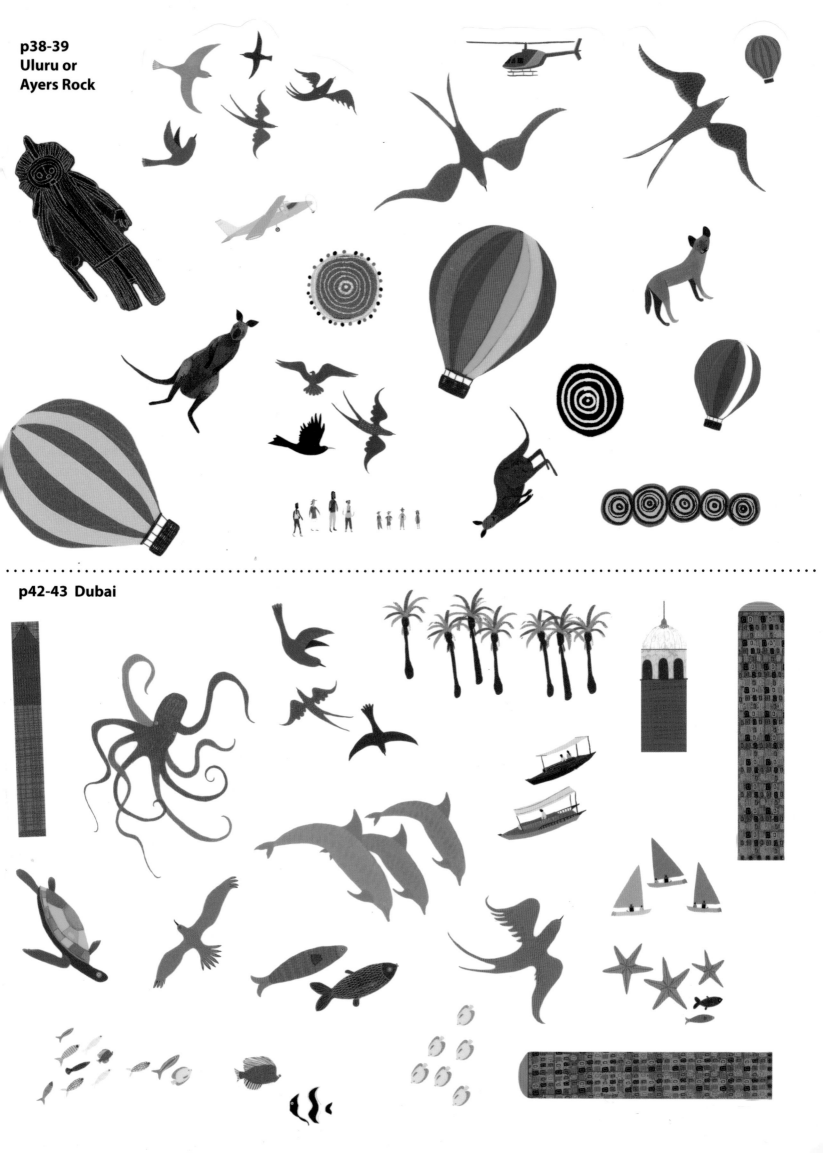

**p38-39
Uluru or
Ayers Rock**

**p42-43 Dubai**